Tommy Tell-Truth

Childrens Holidays

A Poem for Christmas, Easter and Whitsuntide

Tommy Tell-Truth

Childrens Holidays
A Poem for Christmas, Easter and Whitsuntide

ISBN/EAN: 9783742812216

Manufactured in Europe, USA, Canada, Australia, Japa

Cover: Foto ©Andreas Hilbeck / pixelio.de

Manufactured and distributed by brebook publishing software (www.brebook.com)

Tommy Tell-Truth

Childrens Holidays

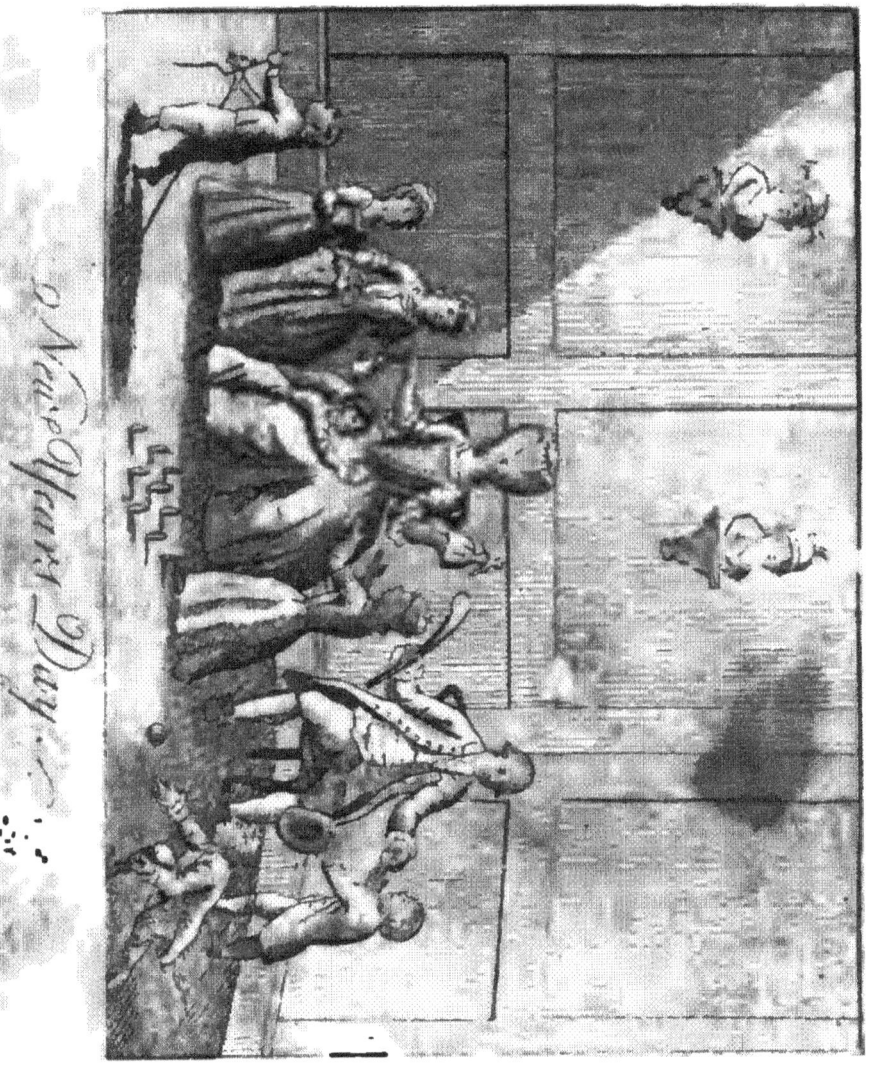

New Years Day

Childrens Holidays:
A POEM
For CHRISTMAS, EASTER, and
WHITSUNTIDE:

Written for the Amusement and Instruction of all the GOOD Masters and Misses in the known World.

To which is added, in Prose, a particular Account of those three happy Festivals; never before printed, and now extracted from the LILLIPUTIAN LIBRARY.

By TOMMY TELL-TRUTH, B. A.

Adorned with Copper-Plate CUTS.

Here Christmas, Easter, Whitsuntide,
Is shewn at once—the School-boy's Pride;
You'll find the Book is quite complete,
At TURPIN's *sold—in St. John's Street.*

London: Printed for H. TURPIN, No. 104, St. *John's* Street, West Smithfield.
[Price Bound SIX PENCE]

Childrens Holidays:

A POEM.

I.

THE spring, the summer, autumn gone,
Each pleasing prospect past;
What storms and tempests then appear,
With many a dreary blast!

II.

All leafless, then, alas! each tree
    In every grove is seen;
No warbling songsters now are heard,
    To harmonize the scene.

III.

But snow on every mountain's brow,
    All cheerless to the sight;
Each pond in icy fetters bound,
    And cover'd o'er with white.

IV.

To man the seasons may compare,
    The spring is infancy,
When sports and inoffensive toys,
    Are seen in every eye.

V. By

By summer is our youth exprest,
  To manhood drawing on;
Then love, and all its sighs and tears,
  Employ the mind alone.

VI.

By autumn you may see our prime,
  Is evident exprest;
When family concerns you find,
  Preside in every breast.

VII.

When frost bespangles all the plain,
  Then halting age appears;
And winter, with his dreary train,
  But shews us our grey hairs.

In spring, in summer, autumn, try
    To cultivate the mind;
The benefits that flow from thence,
    In winter you will find.

IX.

And now around the blazing hearth,
    The family repairs;
The joke goes round, the simple tale,
    To hush, or ease their cares.

X.

The bellman with his verse is heard;
    How awful is the sound!
Each Saint is told of ancient time,
    And now with glory crown'd.

XI. Tho'

XI.

Tho' plain and simple is the rhyme,
  Yet virtuous is the lay:
Ye youths oft con the moral strain,
  And happy shall you be.

XII.

Each parent, now, with anxious heart,
  Thinks on the absent boy;
When far at school, their youthful time
  In learning they employ.

XIII.

The child, to see the time draw nigh,
  The jocund time of year;
When Christmas brings them holidays,
  And plenty of good cheer.

XIV.

At length the happy time arrives;
    The happy, long-wish'd day;
Each lad looks round with joyous eyes,
    At thoughts of Christmas-play.

XV.

The Services are dealt about,
    The master with them stands;
And every boy attentive seems,
    To hear his kind commands.

XVI.

Mark well, says he, what now I say,—
    Be merry, and be wise;
Be careful in whate'er you do,
    To bless your parents eyes.

XVII. Let

XVII.

Let no false toys your minds delude,
　　Your book remember still;
Avoid the idle, saunt'ring race,
　　For sloth's a cruel ill.

XVIII.

The task I've set, observe with care;
　　And when you come again,
In all your transports I shall share,
　　Nor shall my hopes be vain.

XIX.

So shall you prove my care of you,
　　My duty and intent;
So shall you prove your parents' joy,
　　And crown them with content.

XX.

As different lads, go different ways,
    With tears almost they part;
Each shakes his fellow by the hand,
    With nature's honest heart.

XXI.

Friendship's the balm of human life,
    Our chiefest good below;
May this in every breast increase,
    As upwards still they grow.

XXII.

And when the time to meet again
    Returns, may each fond breast
His fellow clasp, with heart sincere,
    And friendly each be blest.

XXIII. And

XXIII.

And now the coach goes whirling on,
    And see, the servants wait,
With joyful parents at the door,
    Or round the op'ning gate.

XXIV.

Each parent views the darling child;
    And anxious seems to trace
The features formerly they knew,
    In every other's face.

XXV.

The tender kiss, the soft embrace,
    Goes mutually around;
They jump, they toy, and every one,
    Bids joy and mirth abound.

XXVI.

Ye Lords and Dukes, or greater things,
　Ye noble, and ye wife;
Leave, for a while, your graver sports,
　For these before your eyes.

XXVII.

See how they romp and jump about,
　Behold their simple toys;
Behold, and if you can for once,
　Be virtuous as these boys.

XXVIII.

How pleasing is their various sports!
　How eager they pursue
Tops, marbles, just as fancy calls,
　And points to something new!

XXIX.

The wide hall echoes with the noise,
    Yet pleasing is the sound,
When skittles, by the well-aim'd bowl,
    Now rattle on the ground,

XXX.

Whlie some at hoop or blind-man's-buff
    Will pass the time away;
And the pleas'd parents stand around,
    To view the childrens play.

XXXI.

The little misses, too, are seen
    With dolls, and female toys;
For 'tis a hoid'ning silly way,
    To share the sport with boys.

XXXII.

No care have they for other things;
    No hatred, anger, strife;
This is the happiest hour of fate,
    The happiest hour of life.

XXXIII.

Oh! may each hour of life be such;
    As innocent and gay:
May virtue glow in every heart,
    To crown each coming day.

XXXIV.

The day once o'er, to bed they go,
    And sleep, devoid of care;
If dreams disturb, 'tis for next day,
    What pleasures they shall share.

XXXV. Soon

XXXV.

Soon as Aurora shews the day,
    They rise with great delight;
They urge the ball across the plain,
    Then hey! for sports at night.

XXXVI.

Each trick is try'd for frisk and fun,
    Each stratagem pursued;
And various gambols go around,
    All innocent and good.

XXXVII.

Now in a ring, behold they sit,
    Their pastime still in view;
Then questions and commands are found
    And hunt the slipper too.

XXXVIII.

Poor Kitty falls, and breaks her face,
 Oh! terrible difaster;
But this is mended in a trice,
 By help of fticking plaifter.

XXXIX.

But Kitty, pray, in time take heed,
 Beware you fall no more;
For if you fall when woman grown,
 You'll fall to rife no more.

XL.

I mean, if once your virtue falls,
 For that's your only jewel,
Advifed in the youthful fair,
 Be cautious how you do ill.

XLI. Before

XLI.

Before you act obferve to think,
    Be modeft,—banifh pride;
Let virtue reign within your breaft,
    And all your actions guide.

XLII.

The old year gone, the new one come,
    And all is mirth again;
The joyful farmer looks elate,
    His looks his mind explain.

XLIII.

They jeft, they laugh, and romp about,
    Enquire of this and that;
Of Dobbin, and the old grey mare,
    Of Cæfar, or the cat.

XLIV. The

XLIV.

The presents, see, of various sorts,
  To master and to miss;
One shakes the hand with hearty glee,
  And t'other gives a kiss.

XLV.

May, as the day returns again,
  Such pleasures still abound;
And every one as blith and gay,
  For many years be found.

XLVI.

Still innocent, and still as gay,
  As pleasing, and as free;
No other thoughts their minds employ,
  But love and unity.

XLVII. Each

XLVII.

Each bosom glad with honest heart,
 Their wishes all sincere;
From morn to morn, from day to day,
 Their eyes ne'er knew a tear.

XLVIII.

In all their sports of every kind,
 O! be it sport alone;
For should they be too fond of play,
 They'll make their parents mourn.

XLIX.

If o'er the frosty path they go,
 And urge the rapid race;
May health attend them in their play,
 To brighten every face.

       L. Or

L.

Or if the ice-bound pool invites
    To skate, or slide away;
Beware the rest who come behind,
    Or trip you up they may.

LI.

So in life's various race you'll find,
    Tho' smooth you seem to slide;
You quickly may be jostled down,
    By vanity or pride.

LII.

Beware ye youths, beware of both;
    For pride's a horrid sin;
And soon you'll find it grow apace,
    If vanity begin.

LIII.

How many dreadful scenes are shewn,
    Examples not a few,
The woeful havock, pride has made,
    Indeed is nothing new.

LIV.

The world's great master Cæsar fell,
    Alone by fatal pride;
And Philip's warlike son the same,
    And many more besides.

LV.

And you ye youthful blooming fair,
    Ne'er let your bosoms glow
With vanity, ne'er fill your heads,
    Or empty pomp and shew.

LVI. Tho'

LVI.

Tho' charming you to every eye,
    And dear to every breast;
Yet mind you act with prudence, when
    By coxcombs you're addrest.

LVII.

Let not their flattering arts prevail,
    Or touch your tender heart;
For every fool, you'll find it true,
    Will act a villain's part.

LVIII.

Let arts, that still the mind employ,
    Be constant in your thought;
And then you'll give your parents joy,
    And do as good girls ought.

LIX.

To dance, to sing, to act with ease,
    Are parts of education,
And such will each beholder please,
    When suited to your station.

LX.

Yet more essential things than these,
    In riper years you'll find;
Should, if you rightly understand,
    Employ your early mind.

LXI.

The book, the needle, and the pen,
    And all domestic life;
For necessary these you'll find,
    To make a frugal wife.

LXII. Tho'

LXII.

Tho' fortune now may speak you kind,
    And all your hopes stand fair;
Yet the vicissitudes of life,
    You possibly may share.

LXIII.

Then when the clouds of indigence
    Surround the throbbing heart;
With mind elate you'll thank the powers,
    You learned each frugal art.

LXIV.

However pleasing be your air,
    However good your mind;
Yet if misfortune you beset,
    But little good you'll find.

LXV.

Then treasure this within your breast,
 Now e'er it be too late;
Thus shall you, in your early youth,
 Anticipate your fate.

LXVI.

So shall your life, with peace be blest,
 In youth, as well as age;
So shall the rays of pure content,
 Attend your evening stage.

LXVII.

But stop, my muse, the moral lay,
 And tune a sprightly strain;
Twelfth-Day, behold approaches near,
 And with a jovial train.

LXVIII.

Free as the day, behold they rife,
 And as the air, as light;
Yet every one with anxious heart,
 Still wifhes for the night.

LXIX.

Then they expect the hall to ring,
 The glorious cake to view;
The fports of various forts begin,
 The fports, and forrows too.

LXX.

For hurly-burly all the day,
 From this thing unto that,
Thomas, has fly mifchief done,
 Againft the cook, fo fat.

LXXI.

LXXI.

The cook, she strait begins to pout,
 And thinks it is amiss;
But John, her sweetheart soon comes in,
 And sooths her with a kiss.

LXXII.

The lads, they too must have their game
 And laugh at what is done;
And who can say they are to blame,
 'Tis all but Christmas fun.

LXXIII.

The lesser youths they twirl the hoop,
 Or gambol on the green;
At length the shades of night appear,
 To usher in the scene.

LXXIV.

The supper o'er, the cakes brought forth,
 So pleasing to them all;
With flags and streamers it appears,
 Within the spacious hall.

LXXV.

And first the tickets are made out,
 With many a merry name;
One is called this, another that,
 To aid the jovial game.

LXXVI.

Now all the busy hands are try'd,
 In fortune's wishing cap;
Yet ne'er a one at present knows,
 What luck to him may hap.

LXXVII. One

LXXVII.

One chuses king, another knave,
    Another jade or slut;
One laughs, and t'other sulks, alas!
    At what his fortune's cut.

LXXVIII.

But above all that can be shewn,
    In this fantastick scene,
Is that the greasy cook should find,
    Her ticket prove the queen.

LXXIX.

When Kings and Princes go to war,
    What havock they do make;
They cut and hack it all about,
    The world is but a cake.

LXXX.

The sighing peasant views his crop,
　By hostile arms o'er run;
And all his pains, and all his care,
　Are instantly undone.

LXXXI.

Ah! cease ye great, ah! sheath your
　　sword,
　Your spoils for pity cease;
Think of the suff'rings that you cause,
　And let the world have peace.

LXXXII.

And now the sports at last are o'er,
　The holidays are done;
To school each youth must go again,
　Adieu to Christmas fun.

LXXXIII. With

LXXXIII.

With aching heart, each takes his leave,
    And posts away amain;
They wish and sigh for joy and sport,
    'Till Easter comes again.

LXXXIV.

Then hey! again, for breaking up;
    Mirth brightens up each eye;
And now my arduous task is done,
    My little friends good bye.

LXXXV.

Again the friendly muse appears,
    Again displays her skill;
And to your wishes, gives her aid,
    With joy and true good-will.

LXXXVI.

While round the desk, each boy is sat,
    His learning to improve;
Prudence and Wisdom does appear,
    To guide them with their love.

LXXXVII.

Now wide extends the youthful mind,
    By sacred science taught;
And all the great extended page,
    Corrects and guides each thought.

LXXXVIII.

Ah! happy childhood! happy time!
    How innocently gay;
When o'er the versed task you smile,
    And crown the pleasing day.

LXXXIX.

Tho' yet the dreary prospect's seen,
   And wint'ry storms abound,
Yet health awaits each active boy,
   Who roams the hills around.

XC.

Tho' leafless trees, no pleasure shew,
   The stream glides cold along;
Soon shall the sun's reviving beams,
   Give rapture to each song.

XCI.

Then shall each youth more chearful be,
   And hail the coming year;
Each bird invite, each flowret gay,
   In all its pride appear.

XCII.

But Shrove-tide bids the clownish train,
    In aukward gambols join;
Yet pray, to throw at cocks, my dear,
    So cruel never join.

XCIII.

From whence it comes, this barb'rous sport
    There's few I think can say;
To hurt a harmless fowl indeed,
    Can never be call'd play.

XCIV.

When Peter did his LORD deny,
    The cock was heard to crow;
Yet that's no reason that you should,
    At him direct the blow.

XCV.

All inoffensive was his voice,
    No harm from him could rise;
No;—'twas ordained so above,
    By him who rules the skies.

XCVI.

The cock with chearful notes awakes,
    The shepherd in the morn;
True as the clock, his herd around,
    To hail the coming dawn.

XCVII.

But now what solemn days are found,
    How serious to the view;
Lent comes;—when in the wilderness,
    CHRIST fasted long for you.

XCVIII.

He wept, he pray'd, he sigh'd, implor'd,
  Nor wept nor pray'd in vain;
For by his suff'ring on the cross,
  He banish'd all your pain.

XCIX.

Deceitful foes his ways beset,
  A Judas him betray'd;
Caught in the snare, he must submit,
  A snare was for him laid!

C.

The dread tribunal is decreed,
  He dies upon the cross;
Rejoice, oh earth!—that thus he dy'd,
  You live but from his loss.

CI. This

CI.

This day GOOD FRIDAY yet is call'd,
  When wide resounds each cry;
Cross bun, all hot, come out with speed,
  Make haste, and come and buy.

CII.

The cross that seals this holy bun,
  Keep still within your mind;
That from that thought, when you shall die,
  Salvation you may find.

CIII.

Thus learning and religion too,
  Shall make you good and wise;
And thro' each varied scene on earth,
  More pure you may arise.

CIV. But

CIV.

But now behold the jocund spring,
   Leads on her happy train;
When buds adorn each spreading tree,
   And flowrets grace the plain.

CV.

The primrose trembles on the bank,
   The violet near is seen;
The cowslip mingles round about,
   Among the fertile green.

CVI.

The lambkin gambols o'er the mead,
   The shepherd in the dale;
With mirth and music, join the dance,
   Or tell the happy tale.

CVII.

And many a youth, and many a maid,
    With innocence, are gay;
Within the straw thatch'd cot are bless'd,
    To pass the time away.

CVIII.

Old Joan and Derby seek the door,
    And seat them on the grass;
Once more well pleas'd to view the spring
    How sweet the moments pass.

CIX.

High soars the lark, to meet the sun,
    Sweet warbling thro' the skies;
So should each little boy and girl,
    In goodness still arise.

CX.

The wood-lark whistles thro' the grove,
    The linnet joins his lay;
The black-bird sounds his notes aloft,
    All nature round is gay.

CXI.

While thus the prospect does appear,
    Delightfully and fine;
Think that the spring is like to youth,
    To goodness thus incline.

CXII.

Rise with the lark, to hail thy GOD,
    'Tis him each blessing gives;
Thro' his benevolence and love,
    It is each mortal lives.

CXIII.

But Easter now draws on a-pace,
    A very pleasant time;
And mark'd with a distinguish'd note,
    By many a holy rhime.

CXIV.

The LORD was crucified, and dead,
    Descended into hell;
And there for three days he remain'd,
    As his Apostles tell.

CXV.

But then again the LAMB arose,
    And did to heaven ascend;
That with his father he might prove,
    Each fallen mortal's friend.

CXVI.

Raise then your voice to him on high,
    To him each praise afford;
He is our only hope below,
    Our great and mighty LORD.

CXVII.

To crown this happy festival,
    Each school-boy now is free;
With cakes and ale, each one is gay,
    And all is mirth and glee.

CXVIII.

Home to their parents they return,
    Their friends, relations too;
When each his task as gladly shews,
    To prove what he can do.

CXIX. The

CXIX.

The taylor brings the new-made suit,
    All pleasing to behold;
And if that Jackey has been good,
    His hat is laced with gold.

CXX.

Then mamma gives the tender kiss,
    And hugs her darling boy;
The father views his comely face,
    And smiles parental joy.

CXXI.

The tender look, the soft reply,
    The smile that gives delight;
The fancied toy, the gilded book,
    Gives rapture to the sight.

CXXII. From

CXXII.

From all around enquiries come,
    Pray how does master Billy;
But if he has not learn'd his book,
    Indeed he'll look but silly.

CXXIII.

'Tis learning which must make you wise
    To learning then attend;
You'll find in time it is your best,
    Your chief and only friend.

CXXV.

Now round about the town they go,
    Each pleasing sight to see;
From this to that, now here now there,
    And all to pleasure thee.

CXXVI. Then

CXXVI.
Then, sir, you must such kindness prize,
    Your friends and parents love;
Who to oblige you, try so much,
    Their tenderness to prove.

CXXVII.
Good eating is at Easter found,
    With pies and roast meat rare;
And every little boy who's good,
    Will surely have his share.

CXXVIII.
Thus having put the Easter o'er,
    To school you must away;
To study wisdom's book again,
    Then come another day.

CXXIX. O'er

CXXIX.

O'er hill, o'er dale, along the road,
    The coachman drives along;
The merry warblers tune the lay,
    Each school boy joins the song.

CXXX.

And now again at school theyre found,
    Intent their book to learn;
From whence they will much knowledge [find
    And every truth discern.

CXXXI.

Sweet is the murmur of the school,
    The conning lesson sweet;
Sweet is the face of ev'ry child.
    In goodness that's compleat.

CXXXII.

The morn that bids the lark arise,
 And hail the God of day;
Bids them alike their lids unclose,
 To study and to pray.

CXXXIII.

The master views his harmless band,
 And deals instructions round;
And tell me where can be a task,
 That's more delightful found.

CXXXIV.

Thus on they go from day to day,
 And ev'ry day improve;
In wisdom as they thus increase,
 They win each person's love.

CXXXV.

Thus roll the infant years away,
    E'er cares the mind invade,
And the long train of human woe,
    Is to their sight display'd.

CXXXVI.

The hoop that rolls along the plain,
    The ball that flies with speed;
The whirling top, or little taw,
    Their pleasure is decreed.

CXXXVII.

Each inoffensive sport and play,
    Brings rapture unaloy'd;
And every day, and every night,
    Fills up the happy void.

CXXXVIII.

But when to man's eftate they rife,
    How chang'd, alas! the fcene;
The paffion urge them to the gore,
    And horrors intervene.

CXXXIX.

Along the tide of life they fteer,
    While billows round them roar;
Without an oar to guide their way,
    Or help them to the fhore.

CXL.

Love, tyrant of the human breaft,
    Sends forth the venom'd dart;
And with a pleafing pain at once,
    Invades the tender heart.

Mad Jealoufy, is feen to rife,
    All frantic,—then defpair;
Surrounds at once, the victim's head,
    Keen hate, and trembling fear,

CXLII.

But why fhould we anticipate
    The ills as yet unfeen;
Ah! let the fportive children play,
    Along the level green.

CXLIII.

And once again let us purfue,
    The little joys they prize;
Bring forth the holidays again,
    Which brightens up their eyes.

CXLIV. Yes,

CXLIV.

Yes, Whitfuntide is coming on,
  To give each heart delight;
The coach shall call them to away,
  And every joy excite.

CXLV.

Huzza! my boys, to town you go,
  Your parents blyth to view;
Joy gives delight to all around,
  To have a sight of you.

CXLVI.

Now bright Pomona shews her sweets,
  Behold where they expand;
Currants and goosberries are seen,
  To tempt each buyer's hand.

CXLVII.

The cherry plump and juicy too,
    Is likewise to be found;
You'll hear them cried thro' ev'ry street
    Black hearts all round and found.

CXLVIII.

But let us trace the scented mead,
    Where all are blyth and gay;
You'll find it a delicious treat,
    To smell the new mow'd hay.

CXLIX.

But what is Whisun-tide you'll say,
    What meaning does it bear;
The question I must grant is right,
    And what you now shall hear.

CL.

It was that sacred time we're told,
    When cloven tongues appear'd;
And o'er each bless'd apostle's head,
    Their sacred influence rear'd.

CLI.

In every tongue it bad them speak,
    To every nation round;
And murm'ring strangers wonder'd all,
    To hear the solemn sound.

CLII.

Then let us hail the sacred day,
    With decent joy and mirth;
Since Heaven has given his mercy so,
    To bless the Son of earth.

[54]
CLIII.

Thus Christmas, Easter, Whitsuntid,
    To you I have fully shewn;
Now all the joy is thus display'd,
    You all may make your own.

CLIV.

Farewell, my little friends farewell,
    I now must bid adieu;
Perhaps when Christmas comes again,
    My theme I may renew.

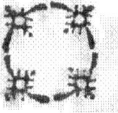

REMARKS

Miss Brinkworth
Everingham
Mansfield

REMARKS ON
CHRISTMAS Holidays.

IT wanted but a few days to this great and solemn festival, when the little society of young gentlemen belonging to a country boarding school, received the joyful tidings of breaking up.—This was agreeable news indeed, and not one but what felt his heart jump for joy at the signal.

For every one must allow that young people ought to have some relaxation from study, in order to make them fonder of learning, when they come to it again, and they that are good ought

ought to meet with every indulgence; and such children as are placed at school, some miles from London, should have some opportunities of seeing their parents and friends, to partake with them some amusements which are customary at Christmas.

After breaking up day was over, which had afforded them much mirth, in the various sports and plays that youth delight in, and every little gentleman had received his piece, which he had written against the time, they waited in expectation of being sent for to their respective homes.

Master Billy Good-boy, asked his little friend, master Tommy Tell-truth, what Christmas was? I will tell you, said

said Tommy, as well as I can.——"It is the day on which our Blessed Lord and Saviour was born, to save us from our sins.—And his birth was told to some shepherds who were feeding their flocks;—who with great joy left their sheep, and were led by a star that appeared in the east, which went before them, till it came over against the manger where CHRIST lay, with his mother the Virgin Mary."

Now this was a very pretty account from such a little boy, and shewed he loved his book, or he would not have known so much.——Well says Billy, I think we can do no less than keep his birth-day, as you know we most of us keep our own.——Very true, says Tommy, but at the same time we ought to take

take care that our mirth is innocent, we may eat roaſt beef, and plumb-pudding, with plenty of minced pies and other good cheer, and have a fine twelfth cake to chuſe king and queen, without doing any harm to ourſelves or any body elſe.——We may viſit all our friends and acquaintance, and have them to ſee us, and join in many different harmleſs plays.—aye, that we will, ſays Billy, huzza! then they run to the reſt of the lads, and all of them together gave a general holloo—huzza!

The next day ſome were fetched away in coaches, ſome in chaiſes, ſome on horſeback, and others went in different ſtages; and a very agreeable ſight it was to ſee them one by one take leave of his maſter, and receive proper inſtructions

instructions to behave themselves, and get the task assigned them while away, which they might easily do without hindering their pleasures.—Which we will leave them to pursue without entering any further on the subject, as a more particular account of Christmas diversions will be found in the poetical part of this work.

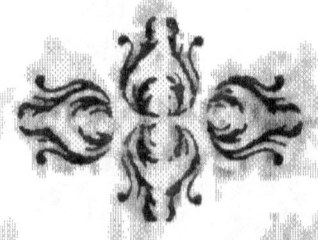

REMARKS ON EASTER Holidays.

AFTER winter's dark and dreary feaſon is over, the ſpring begins to advance; when the graſs ſprings up, and the buds and flowers appear again, giving us a pleaſing proſpect of ſummer, ſlowly advancing.

Youth is a proper emblem of ſpring, which is to grow up and be covered with learning; bloſſoms, which in time will ripen into the choiceſt of fruit.

Eaſter holidays being come, all the young ladies and gentlemen at different ſchools are preparing to return to their friends for a little while, every one having

having been as studious as possible to let them see how they have advanced in their education, that they might not think they had idled away their time, and put them to such expence for nothing.

The young gentlemen had written curious pieces on the occasion, and the young ladies had worked samplers and and other fine work, each striving to excel, that she might have the praise of her governess.

It is reasonable to suppose, that most young folks will enquire what the custom was for keeping Easter holidys?— But if they read the Scripture it will inform them, that our Blessed SAVIOUR arose again from the dead, after he had lain

lain in the sepulchre three days, for he was crucified on Good Friday by the Jews, because they would not believe that he was the True CHRIST, but an Impostor, as they expected the Son of GOD would come in great splendor to reign over them, and be their king; and as he was born in a manger, and was always meek and lowly, they would not believe in him:—but the grave could not hold him long, he rose again and ascended into heaven, which is the reason we ought to rejoice, as he is now at the right hand of GOD making intercession for us.

Perhaps it may be said by some, there is no reason for children to leave their school at these holidays, as there is no plumb-pudding nor minced pies in season now, but what of that, there are other

other things as good, but above all, the
fight of one's parents and friends, is
worth having a few holidays for.

Besides, when children are good and
dutiful, and mind their learning, the
least they can be indulged in is to break
up four times a year, to take a little
pleasure.

Therefore according to annual custom, we shall dismiss them a little while,
hoping at the same time they will not
forget to learn their tasks, that they may
be received with pleasure by their master and governesses, when they come
back again to school.

And now hey for home—away they
drive, their friends meet them with
open arms, and when they get home

present

prefent them with many pretty toys, and take them abroad with them where ever they go, and to be fure they muſt be admired when they have taken pains to make themſelves accompliſhed.

REMARKS

On Whitsuntide.

THIS holiday took its name from White Sunday, a day, when according to antient custom, people used to put on white robes.

It was likewise the day of Pentecost, when the spirit descended like cloven tongues, as mentioned in the scripture.

And now for another breaking up time, and going to see friends; who would not strive hard to learn when they are at school, when they have so many opportunities of taking their pleasure.

Now

Now indeed is the pleasantest time of the year, the fields and gardens are in their highest beauty, the hay-makers are at work which is grateful to the sight and smell—oh how pleasant it is to walk among the cocks, or to sit down on them to rest when one is tired.

How delightful to the taste, at this season is the ripened fruit, and wholesome too, if eaten with discretion; but some children are so eager of it that they get a surfeit;—beware of that, as it has been fatal to many a pretty youth, therefore be careful, and make use of reason and moderation in all you do.

At this time likewise, most young people have new cloaths, and I would advise them to keep them as clean as possible

possible, that when they go back again to school, they may have the credit of them.

Some children are so slovenly or sluttish, that they can't wear any thing above a week before it is spoiled, but every young lady or gentleman should always appear clean and neat, and never tear their cloaths, unless by accident, which very seldom happens if they play at proper games.—But some are naturally so wild, they will not be under any restraint, but run and rant about so, that they tear their things off their backs, and their skin into the bargain.

However we shall say no more of this now, as they are going to enjoy

joy the Whitsun holidays, and we hope they will have a great deal of pleasure.

The Papas have provided hobby horses, and many other curious things for their sons, as they have heard a good account of them from their masters;—— and the mammas have provided dolls and baby houses and other things for their little daughters, all is to be pleasure and happiness on every side.

These things are for the very young ones, those that are older and of consequence above such things, no doubt will meet with proper encouragement from their parents, as a reward of their well doing.

And

[69]

And now they are going to set out I will take my leave of them, wishing them a good journey, and a happy meeting on all sides.

A COLLECTION OF LETTERS

From Several PRETTY MASTERS and MISSES, TO THEIR PARENTS:

BEING

A SPECIMEN of their FORWARDNESS in LEARNING:

Now FIRST made PUBLIC, For the IMITATION of OTHERS.

By TOMMY TELL-TRUTH.

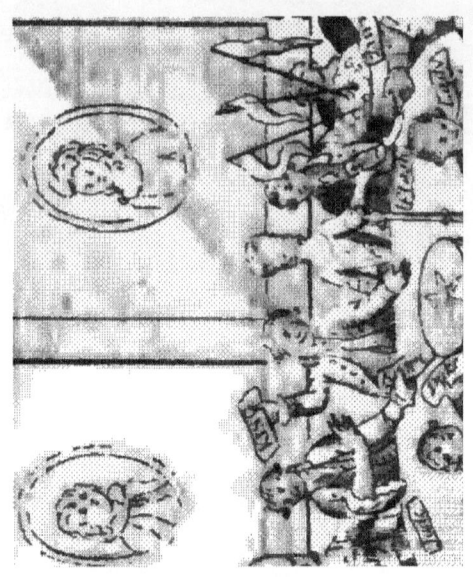

DEDICATION.

LETTER I.

To Sir T. Tell-Truth, Jun.

Worthy Sir,

YOUR conſtant attention to your learning, the ſweet temper and amiable deportmeut in all things, has determined me to make choice of you for a Patron, to this collection of Juvenile Epiſtles, not doubting but you will recommend it to all your little Intimates, and likewiſe to your honoured Parents, who,

who I dare say, will not be a little pleased at the perusal of some of these little performances, the hopes of which and pleasing you, first prompted me to this Publication. I am, SIR,

Your most dutiful,

and humble Servant,

T. TELL-TRUTH.

LETTER II.

To Sir WIDLIAM WORTHY,

Dear Sir,

THE time now draws nigh to to that part of the year, so pleasing to every good boy, I mean Christmas; for then I shall have the pleasure of beholding my dear Parents, which will be more pleasing to me than all the joys of breaking up, not but that affords a great deal of mirth, such as burning the rod breaking the ferule, and other particulars not worthy to mention, yet all attended generally with repeated shouts of applause; but amidst these

joys

joys, I have still a dread, left you should think I have been of a truant disposition, yet can assure my dear Pappa and Mamma, I have not, my Master compliments me so far as to say I take my learning very fast, and that I shall be a good Scholar, I hope I shall prove his words true, not only for your satisfaction, but likewise for my own, as I must own, I have a a great desire for knowledge; pray let me hear from you soon, and inform me how my dear Mamma and Sister and Brothers do, for I long to hear; I should like to hear from you every day, and since I am now grown capable of writing, I shall be always
sending

sending to you, and hope you will not think me impertinent; pray accept of my duty to you and Mamma, give my love to all friends, and believe me, dear Pappa,

    Your dutiful Son,

       W. WORTHY.

LETTER

LETTER III.

To Thomas Goodwill, Esq.

Dear Pappa,

CHRISTMAS is now come, and to-morrow we shall embark to see our Parents, some one way, and some another; some with light hearts, and some with heavy; you may be surprized perhaps, to think that any should be reluctant to see their Friends and Parents; but indeed we have some very bad boys, who are so fond of play, that they will neglect their books, and if they can, get others to do their tasks; I

am

am quite aſhamed of ſuch things, and have never, thank GOD, been the leaſt remiſs in that article, or any other, incumbent on a good child, as I hope the Letters from my Maſter, and my own behaviour, when you ſee me, will convince you of; you will receive this not long before my arrival, when I ſhall have the happineſs of beholding what is more dear to me than all the world, my Parents. My Couſin Tommy Gentle, deſires to be remembered to you, as he is obliged to go another way; upon my word, Pappa, he is a very good boy, and is very fond of his book, and I dare ſay, will be a great
ſatisfaction

satisfaction to his friends and relations, as he is to me.

Pray abcept of my duty,

T. GOODWILL.

LETTER

LETTER IV.

To Mrs. LOVEWORTH.

Honoured Mamma,

I Have the pleasure to inform you, that I arrived safe at School on the 15th Instant, I must confess I was very melancholy all the Journey, after parting from my dear Mamma, and all those pleasing trifles I enjoyed during the Christmas Holidays; but though you are still uppermost in my thoughts, yet the manner I was received by my Governess, and the rest of my school acquaintance, has greatly alleviated my sorrows on that account; our evenings are taken up with the relation of what has happened during our abfence from each other, and I am not a little pleafed to find my entertainment was not inferior to any of them; by their own acsounts, Mifs Kitty Wilful returned ill-humoured, the reafon of which is, as far as I can learn, fhe was greatly chid for her neglect in learning; indeed fhe never minded any thing but toys and drefs, nay, fhe could not bear to fee any one better dreffed than herfelf, and if it was in her power, would ftrive to injure them at any rate, fuch was her fpirit of envy; thank God, I am not of that difpofition, nor never fhall I hope;

hope; those excellent lessons, which your example in life, as well as precepts to me, will always be sufficient to deter me from ever being proud, insolent, or vain. Pray excuse this tedious and unconnected epistle, and believe I am,

Your very dutiful Daughter,

JANE LOVEWORTH.

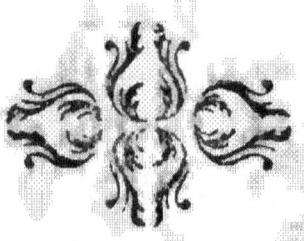

LETTER V.

To Sir RICHARD WEALTHY.

Dear Sir,

SINCE I have left you and my honoured Mother, I have been extremely happy considering the want of your presence, which must be always dear to me; my former play-mates are pretty near all returned, and those that are absent we do not expect again, as when they were here they were so idle and such dunces as to be hated by the Master, and despised by all the rest of the school; Billy Fribble and Charles Bounce especially; indeed they were not fit to
be

among good boys, for they were for ever endeavouring to perſuade the reſt of the boys to come into their ſilly and idle ways, but they never yet drew me into their ſnare, and I am determined never ſhall; indeed I thought once their Friends were more kind to them than you to me, as they were always ſending them money and preſents, but I find ſuch indulgences are only calculated to ruin, inſtead of being of ſervice to young minds; my old ſchool-fellow Maſter Fairdeal, has had an eſtate left him by his Uncle, from the good character he always heard of him,

from

from which I find your words are very true, That good behaviour rewards itself. Pray, Pappa, remember me to all Friends, and accept of my duty to Mamma and yourself,

and believe me sincerely your Son,

R. WEALTHY.

FINIS.

A Catalogue of Entertaining Books for Children (each adorned with Copper Plate and other Cuts, bound and gilt) printed for H. Turpin, No. 104, St. John's Street, West-Smithfield.

1 History of Fanny Fairchild and Charlotte Jones, 1d.
2 History of Tommy Sugar Plumb, 1d.
3 History of Polly Cherry, 1d.
4 Pappa's Present to his good Children, 1d.
5 Nancy Cock's Golden Toy, 2d.
6 Instructive and Entertaining Emblems, by Miss Thoughtful, 2d.
7 The English Scholar's Magazine, 2d.
8 Turpin's London Primer, 3d.
9 A Pretty Play Book, 4d.
10 An Alphabetical History of the Bible, 4d.
11 Adventures of Roderick Random, 6d.
12 Adventures of Gulliver's Travels, 6d.
13 Ditto neatly Coloured, 9d.
14 History of Don Quixote, 6d.
15 Ditto neatly Coloured, 9d.
16 Æsop's Fables, Cuts, 6d.

17 Ditto

17 Ditto Cuts neat in Red, 9d.
18 Mirror of Amusement, or Happy Village, 6d.
19 Ditto neatly Coloured, 9d.
20 Description of Birds, Beasts, Fishes, and Insects, 6d.
21 Ditto neatly Coloured, 9d.
22 Little Masters and Misses Delight, 6d.
23 Ditto neatly Coloured, 9d.
24 Chrildrens Holidays, a Poem, 6d.
25 Ditto neatly Coloured, 9d.
26 Bartholomew Fair, 6d.
27 Ditto neatly Coloured, 9d.
26 Select Moral Tales, 6d.
29 Young Moralist, 6d.
30 Ditto neatly Coloured, 2s. 6d.
31 Todd's new and compleat Spelling Book, adorned with Cuts, 1s.
32 Todd's History of the New Testament, 1s. 6d.
33 Marshall's Spelling Book with Cuts, the 4th. Edition, 1s.
34 Marshall's Arithmetic, 1s.
35 History of Prince Almanzor and the Beautiful Shepherdefs, 6d.
36 Marshall's Sentimental Mystery, a Set of Cards for Amusement and Moral Instruction, 1s.

37 The Poetical Looking Glaſs, a Set of Cards, by Bob Short, 1s.
38 The Rural Chriſtian, a Deſcriptive Poem, with Copper Plates, by G. Wright, Eſq. 3s
39 Walking Amuſements, in Proſe and Verſe, Moral and Entertaining, with a Map of the Roads to Heaven and Hell, 3s.
40 Thoughts in younger Life, in Proſe and Verſe, by G. Wright, Eſq. 3s.
41 Solitary Walks for Young Gentlemen and Ladies, in the Stile of Hervey's Meditations, 3s.
42 The Chriſtian's Coat of Arms, a large and elegant Engraving, with Explanations, 1s
43 Harlequin and the Goaler, a Turn-up, 6d.
44 Collombine taking Leave, a Turn-up, 6d.
45 Turpin's Drawing Book of Landſcapes, 6d.
46 Watch Prints, King George II. 3d.
47 ——— King George III. 3d.
48 ——— Queen Charlotte, 3d
49 ——— Mr. Beard, and Miſs Brent, 3d.
50 ——— The Pretty Dancer, 3d.
51 ——— The Wanton Dreamer, 3d.
52 ——— The Shepherd and Sepherdeſs, 3d.
53 Sundry of Darley's Humourous and Maſonry Prints, each Print 6d

54. Bettesworth's English Grammar Epitomized, much in Repute, for the Use of Schools, 6d
55. Bettesworth's Collections of Tables, 2d.
56. Arithmetic Made Easy, 2d.

In the Press, and speedily will be published, sundry other Entertaining Books for Children.

Where likewise may be had the following Books, printed for H. TURPIN.

1. ARGAR's Young Engineer's best Assistant, in a Treatise on Fortifications, with Copper Plates, 8vo. sewed, 5s.
2. Crakelt's New and Compleat Treatise of Spherical Trigonometry, carefully translated from the French of Mr. Mauduit, 8vo. with Plates, sewed, 4s.
3. Hutton's Principles on Bridges, with Figures, 8vo. Sewed, 2s. 6d.
4. Harris's Types of all the Visible Eclipses to the Year 1800, Dedicated to Earl Spencer, Viscount Althorp, neatly Engraved, 2s. 6d

5 God's

5 God's Revenge against Murder and Adultery, remarkably displayed in 30 Tragical Histories, shewing the Justice and Power of Divine Providence in punishing such atrocious Offences; newly revised & corrected, by the Rev. P. Batteson, embellished with 31 Copper Plates, representing upwards of 100 remarkable Passages in the History, 4to. calf, lettered, 10s. 6d.

6 Hervey's Meditations, 2 vol. Crown 8vo. large Print, with Copper Plates 6s.

7 Ross's View of all Religions in the Known World, New Edition, by the Rev. Mr. Entick, 8vo. Sewed, 6s.

8 Ray's Collection of English and Scotch Proverbs, 8vo. Bound, 6s.

9 West's Scripture Sufficiency, practically demonstrated, 12mo. Bound, 2s.

10 Miss Rolt's Miscellaneous Poems, 1s.

11 Young's Compleat Grazier & Farmer's Universal Assistant, to which is added the Compleat Vermin-killer, 12mo. Sewed, 1s.

12 Bland's Dignity of the Christian Priesthood, Dedicated to the Abp. of Canterbury, 8vo. Sewed, 2s.

13 Poems on several Occasions, by John Bennett, a Journeyman Shoemaker, 8vo. sewed, 2s. 6d.
14 Smith's Christianity Unmasked, or unavoidable Ignorance, preferable to corrupt Chistianity, a Poem, in 21 Cantos, 8vo sewed, 4s.
15 Whites Compleat Guide to the Management of Bees, 8vo. Boards 2s. 6d.
16 Bianca, a Tragedy, by R. Shepherd, 8vo. Sewed, 1s. 6d.
17 Michael Smith's Twelve Sermons, on several Occasions, 8vo. Sewed, 3s. 6d.
18 Haddon Smith's Twelve Sermons on the most interesting Subjects of the Christian Religion, 8vo. in Boards, 3s. 6d.
19 Poems, Religious, Moral, and Entertaining, by Mrs. Collier, who wrote an Answer to Stephen Duck, the Thresherman's Labourer; called the Washer-woman's Labour. 1s.
20 Peyton's History of English Language, 1s.
21 Bunyan's Pilgrim's Progress, with his Grace abounding to the Chief of Sinners, new Editions with Copper Plates, 8vo. 6s.

www.ingramcontent.com/pod-product-compliance
Lightning Source LLC
Chambersburg PA
CBHW021948160426
43195CB00011B/1277